525
BR

Branley, Franklyn M.

A book of planet
Earth for you

DATE			
T12			
T19			
T-21			
T8			
T13			
T20			
79			

A

**A Book of
Planet Earth for you
Branley, Franklyn
E 525 BRA/Not AR**

a book of
Planet Earth
for you

a book of
Planet Earth for you

by Franklyn M. Branley

illustrated by Leonard Kessler

Thomas Y. Crowell Company   New York

ALSO BY FRANKLYN M. BRANLEY

AND ILLUSTRATED BY LEONARD KESSLER:

Library of Congress Cataloging in Publication Data

Branley, Franklyn Mansfield

A book of planet Earth for you.

SUMMARY: Discusses the appearance of the earth as seen from outer space, some concepts of its shape, its composition and size, and its movements and their effect on ocean and air currents.

1. Earth—Juv. lit. [1. Earth]

I. Kessler, Leonard P. ill. II. Title.

QB631.B693 1975   525   74-30408

ISBN 0-690-00754-X (CQR)

1 2 3 4 5 6 7 8 9 10

a book of
Planet Earth for you

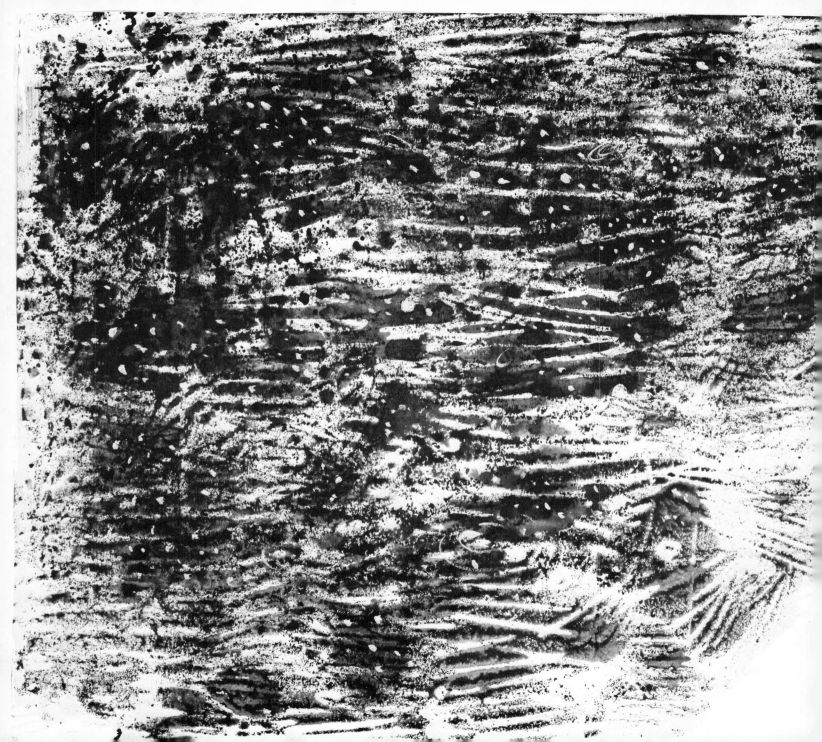

There are millions of stars in the vast universe of which our Solar System is a tiny part. Many of those stars may have planets going around them, the way Earth and Venus and Mars and the other planets in our Solar System go around the Sun. And many of those planets may have intelligent life on them.

Let's suppose that there is such a planet out there among the stars. And suppose that the people on that mythical, distant planet—let's call it Omega, and we'll call the people Omegans—have telescopes. If they did not, they would not be able to see any of the planets of our Solar System, although they still could see the Sun as a rather dim star. But if they did have telescopes, and if these were powerful enough—more powerful than any we have—they would see the rings of Saturn. It

would be hard for them to see Mercury, because it is so near the Sun, or Pluto, which is so far from it.

Venus would appear quite bright to them; so would Jupiter. They would notice that the polar caps of Mars grew large at times, then grew smaller. They would see that the color of the planet changed from greenish to brownish as the Martian seasons changed. The Omegans would see little change in Uranus and Neptune from day to day, month to month, or year to year.

They would observe that our planet, the third planet from the Sun, changed a lot. Sometimes it would be quite blue. At other times it would appear white. The Omegans would understand the meaning of these color changes on Earth, for their own planet would also have water and clouds upon it.

They would see that our planet was one of a family of nine small objects which circled a central star. And they would discover that its yearly journey around that star was more than one thousand million kilometers (584,000,000 miles).

After observing the planet and the star it went around for some time, the Omega astronomers would see that the star was moving through space. As it moved it carried along with it the third planet, and all the other planets as well. Most astronomers on Omega would not spend any time looking at this third planet, because it was going around an average and unimportant star, and because of its very small size. But if there was one among them who looked more closely at that small blue-white world, he would see at once that the planet had phases.

Sometimes he could see only a thin sliver of it; sometimes a quarter of it. He would know that the planet was round. This would not surprise him, for practically all objects in space are round. The particles of which they are made are pulled together by gravitation and packed into the smallest possible space. Gravitation packs them into the shape that has the smallest surface for its volume, the shape that results when pressures are the same throughout—a round ball.

The Omega astronomer would also see that this third planet moved in many different ways. When there was a full-Earth, he might select some marking that didn't change, a continent perhaps. He would watch the continent disappear, reappear on the opposite side, move across the planet, then disappear again. By counting the turns he would find that the planet turns $365\frac{1}{4}$ times while it goes around its star. The planet rotates on its axis (the imaginary "axle" that passes from pole to pole), and it revolves around the star.

As the planet rotated, the Omegan would notice that its axis was not straight up and down in relation to the plane of its path through space. He would see that it was tilted at an angle of $23\frac{1}{2}°$. Because of this, the light that fell on different parts of the planet from the central star wasn't always the same. That would account for the changes seen in the color of the planet. The white polar regions occasionally changed in size. Parts of the globe seemed green at some times and brownish-green at other times.

The Omegans would probably figure out that the small number-three planet had gases surrounding it, and they might also find out that the gases were mostly nitrogen and oxygen. The Omegan space program might even send a planet probe to the small world to get a larger view. But chances are they wouldn't bother. There are plenty of larger worlds to explore. Our small planet wouldn't be worth the effort and expense to explore it with a planet-circling probe, or with a probe that might land on the alien world.

MAP
OF WORLD
OF
ANAXIMENES
500 B.C.

Omegans looking at our planet from deep outer space would know things about it that it took us centuries to discover. For example, people of ancient days knew about the parts of the Earth: the water, air, rocks, and soil of which it is made. But they knew very little about the Earth or the sky as a whole.

They thought that Earth was flat. It looked flat to them. They believed the world was a flat place surrounded by high mountains. There were high

MAP OF EARTH 548 A.D.

places you could go to, and low places. But no matter which direction you traveled, you would reach the high mountains that bordered the world. The mountains were so high that no one could hope to climb them. Even if anyone did, there was nothing to be gained. Beyond the mountains there was only the sea. The sea was the outermost boundary of the world. It was the frame within which were the mountains and the flat world.

In ancient times the sky was explained in many ways. Some people believed it was a flat plate supported by four legs, each leg resting on a mountaintop. The stars were lanterns hung from this flat sky. They were lit each night by the gods, and put out with the approach of daylight. Others believed that the sky was a curved metal cover with many holes through it. An observer could look through the holes and see the brightness that lay beyond. The brightness was the place where the gods lived. The greatest of the gods was the Sun. Some people thought that each day a chariot carried the Sun god across the sky from horizon to horizon. When the Sun god was not in the sky a lesser god, the Moon, occupied the region.

These early theories about the Earth were based upon observation: People could see that the stars came on at night and went off during the day and that some stars moved. Perhaps it was the gods who turned them on, or moved them. The Earth was uneven, there were mountains and valleys, but

there was no reason to think it was curved or round like a ball. It was surely flat. Not only did Earth appear that way, but ships that ventured too far into the sea proved it. The ships seemed to fall off the edge of the earth. At least they certainly were seen no more.

If you and I knew no better, we'd think that Earth was flat, too, just as people did long ago. Forget that you know Earth is round, and look down a highway, or a city street, across a lake or down a river. Except for a hill here and there, Earth seems flat. Our senses give us no feeling for the roundness of the Earth. Our view is too limited. But we know that Earth is round. Astronauts have traveled out beyond our planet. They have looked back, and seen it all at once, not just a part of Earth but the entire Earth-ball. Like the mythical Omegans, our astronauts have seen a sphere, a spectacular blue world which is mostly covered with white clouds. Earth is round, all right. There is no question about it.

Even if astronauts had not taken pictures of the Earth, and so proved its roundness, there are many reasons why we know that our Earth must be round.

More than two thousand years ago there was a Greek scientist, Anaximander of Miletus (611–546 B.C.). In ancient days people were known by a personal name and also by the name of the place where they were born. Miletus was a great Greek city some 2,500 years ago.

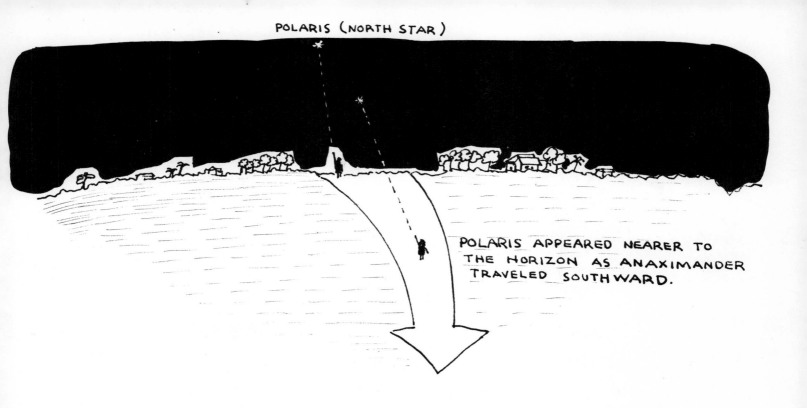

POLARIS (NORTH STAR)

POLARIS APPEARED NEARER TO THE HORIZON AS ANAXIMANDER TRAVELED SOUTHWARD.

Anaximander noticed that when he traveled southward the stars of the north, especially Polaris, seemed to get lower in the sky. As he returned northward, Polaris seemed to get higher in the sky. The Earth must be curved from north to south, he said. If it were not, the stars would always appear the same distance above the horizon. Anaximander

could not make similar observations east and west because the stars and the whole sky moved westward. (He probably did not know why, but we know it was because of Earth's rotation.) The Earth must be a cylinder, Anaximander thought, curved from north to south, but not curved from east to west.

But people who lived at the seashore had a broader view of the Earth. When they watched a ship go out to sea, they noticed that the ship did not disappear by getting smaller and smaller—

becoming a tiny dot. Rather it disappeared while it was still much larger than a dot. And it did not disappear all at once, as it would if it really dropped off the edge of the world. First the hull (the bottom part of the ship) could not be seen, then the deck, and finally the top of the mast. No matter which way it sailed—north, south, east, or west—the ship always disappeared in the same fashion. For this to happen, the earth had to be a sphere, and not a cylinder.

There was another reason why many ancient Greek astronomers could not accept the idea that Earth was a cylinder. They knew that an eclipse of the Moon occurred when Earth's shadow fell on the Moon. Always, this shadow was curved, and the curve was always circular. The only object that always produces a circular curve is a sphere. A cylinder would sometimes make a straight shadow, so Earth could not be a cylinder. It must be a sphere.

Around 500 B.C. Pythagoras of Samos proclaimed that the Earth was round.

About a hundred and fifty years later, Aristotle of Stagira (384–322 B.C.) answered the one big question that people had been asking. If the world is round, they wondered, why don't people on the bottom fall off?

Because, said Aristotle, *down* is toward the center of the Earth. This is true no matter where you are on Earth.

If you were on the Moon, down would be toward the center of the Moon. On Mars, down would be toward the center of Mars. You can't "fall off" Earth, or fall "down" from Earth because there is no up or down in the Solar System. Down is toward the center of each planet, up is away from its center.

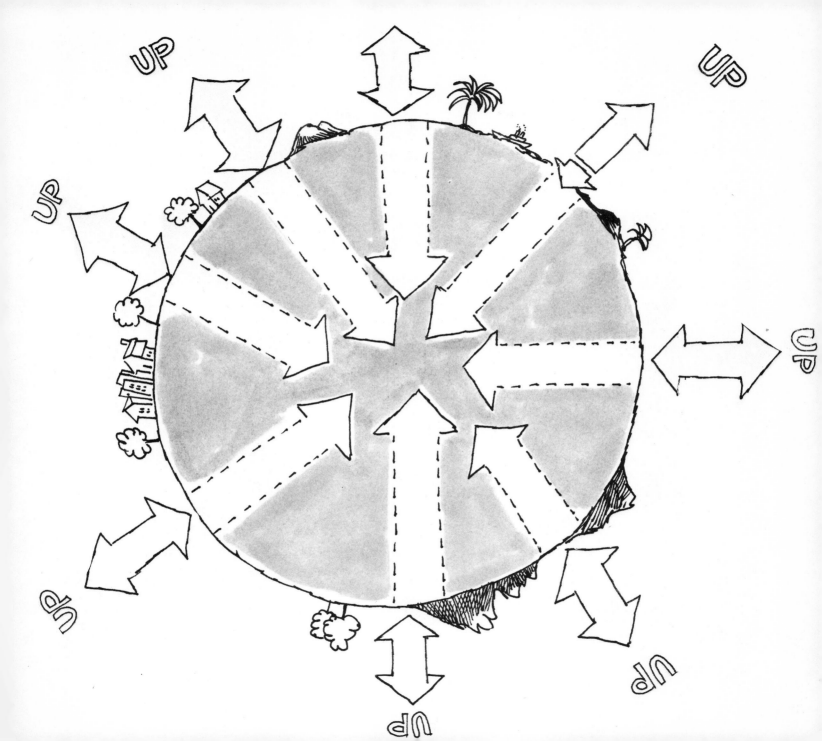

The early Greeks were sure Earth was round, but they could not prove it was so. Not until almost two thousand years later was there proof of the roundness of the Earth. In 1519 Ferdinand Magellan, a Portuguese explorer, set out to sail around the world—starting toward the west and returning from the east. Magellan died on the journey, but in 1522 one of his ships with eighteen men aboard completed the circle, proving that Earth is a round planet.

The journey around the world of one of Magellan's ships also proved that the Earth was much larger than many people had believed. This was the first time anyone had actually gone around the Earth, but another Greek, Eratosthenes of Cyrene (276–196 B.C.), had measured the Earth many hundreds of years earlier.

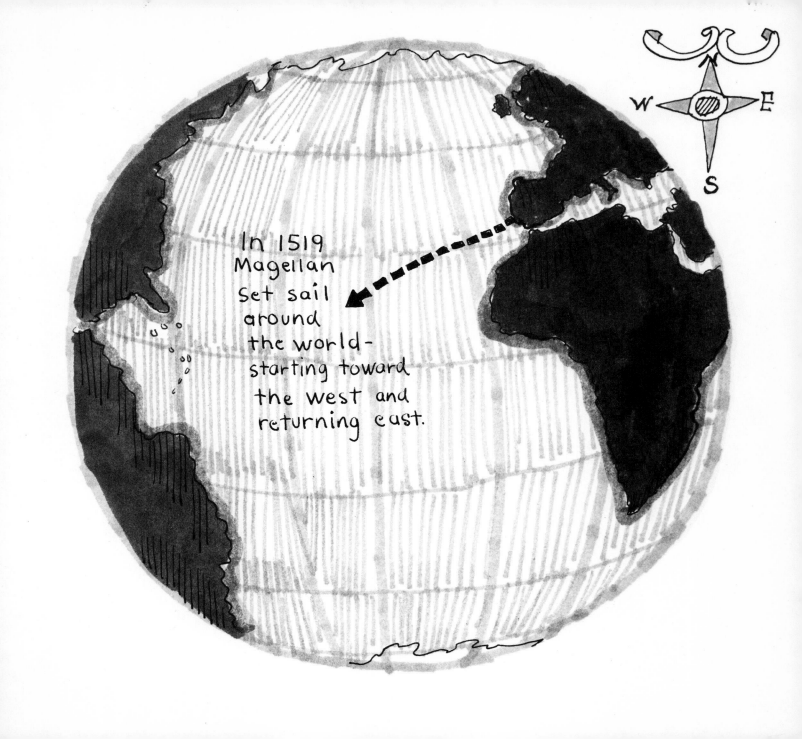

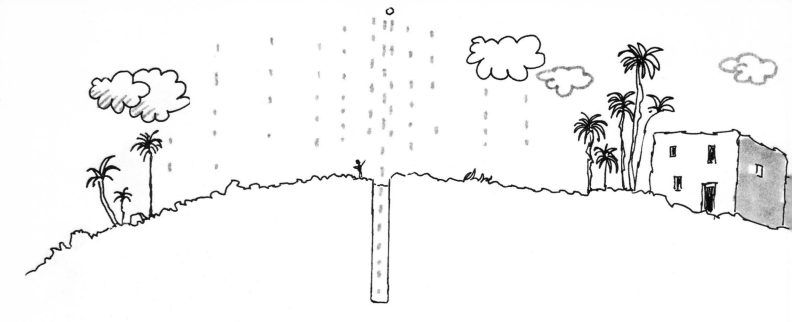

Eratosthenes knew that at Syene (now called Aswan), in the southern part of Egypt, sunlight on a certain day struck the water at the bottom of a deep well at noontime. The day was the first day of summer, the summer solstice, when the Sun had reached its most northerly position. On that day the Sun was directly overhead for an observer at Syene. Incidentally, the well which Eratosthenes had dug especially for this experiment still exists. It is located on the island of Elephantine at Aswan on the Nile River.

The next year, at the same instant—noontime on the first day of summer—Eratosthenes made observations of the position of the Sun from Alexandria. This was a city directly north of Syene. He knew that the Sun was very far away from the Earth, so far away that the sunlight reached Earth in parallel lines.

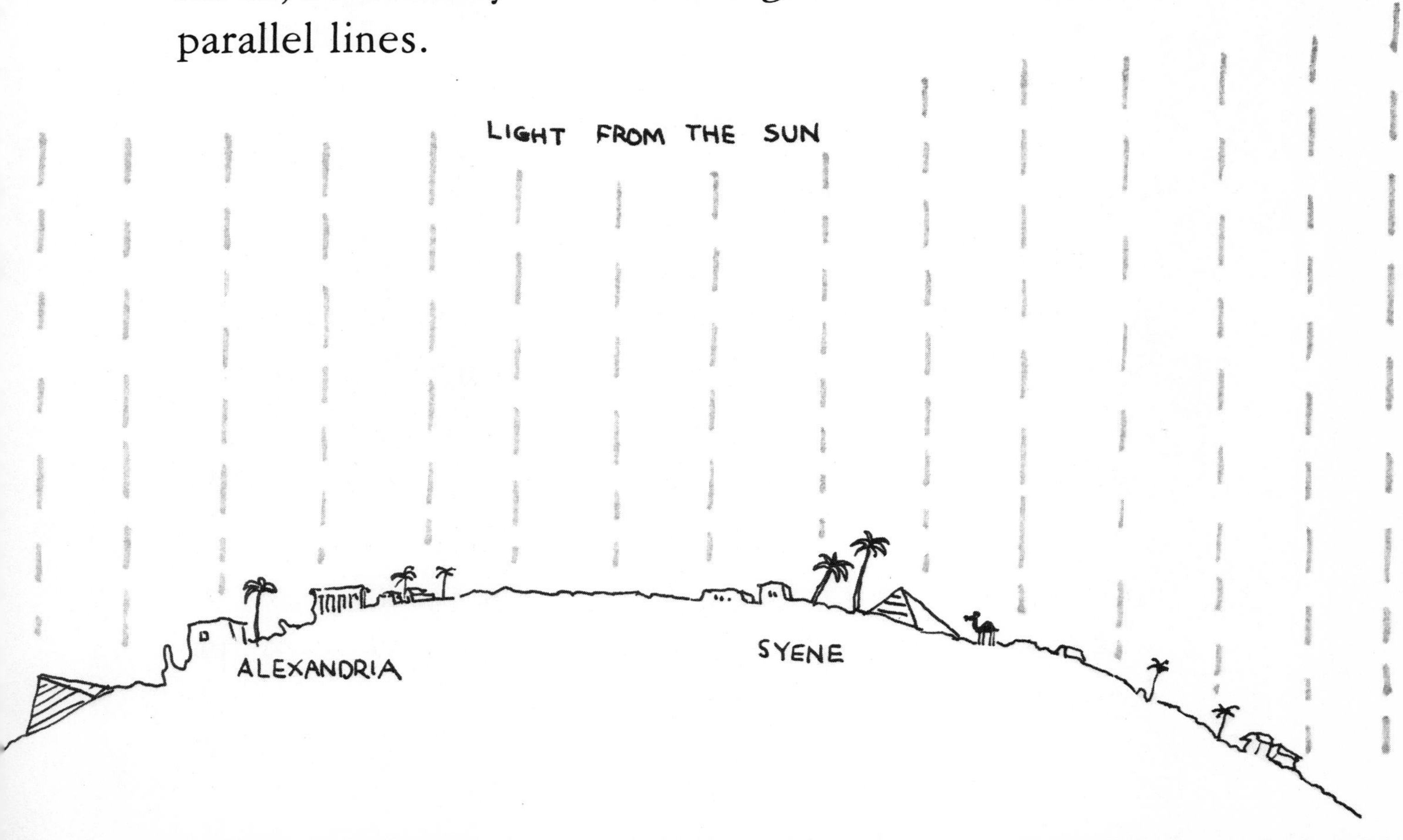

LIGHT FROM THE SUN

ALEXANDRIA

SYENE

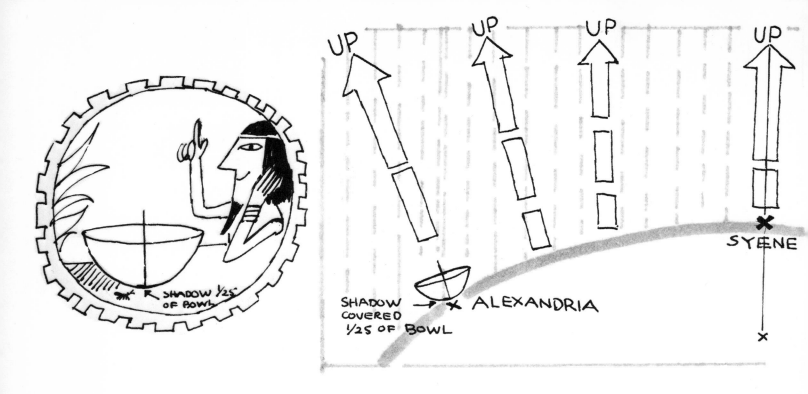

SHADOW 1/25 OF BOWL

SHADOW COVERED 1/25 OF BOWL → X ALEXANDRIA

SYENE

For his observation he used a round bowl, with a needle fixed at the center, pointing straight upward. The needle cast a shadow on the inside surface of the bowl. The shadow, Eratosthenes estimated, covered $1/25$ of the bowl. Since the bowl was one-half of a circle, the shadow covered $1/50$ of the complete circle. If the distance between Syene and Alexandria resulted in a shadow that covered

$^1/_{50}$ of the circle, then the distance around the Earth must be 50 times greater. The distance between the two cities was 5,000 stadia, which made the distance around the Earth 250,000 stadia, later corrected to 252,000.

The stadium was the unit of measurement used by the Greeks—it may have equaled 517 feet. The Earth was a great ball, said Eratosthenes, some 24,650 miles around. And he was right.

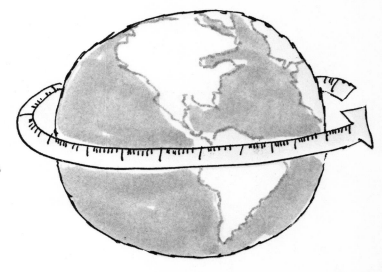

THE DISTANCE AROUND THE EARTH
IS 24,650 MILES OR 252,000 STADIA

Modern-day scientists would know that the Earth must be round even if astronauts had not seen it and Magellan's expedition had not sailed around it. Scientists know this because of their knowledge of physics, and because of theories about how the Earth came into existence.

At one time Earth was a vast swirling cloud of gases and cosmic dust. The gases and dust particles were in constant motion. Eventually separate particles combined with others. A clump of particles resulted. The gravity of the clump pulled in other particles, so that the clump grew larger. It is believed that our planet grew from such a beginning—more and more materials gathered together, the gravitation increasing as the mass increased.

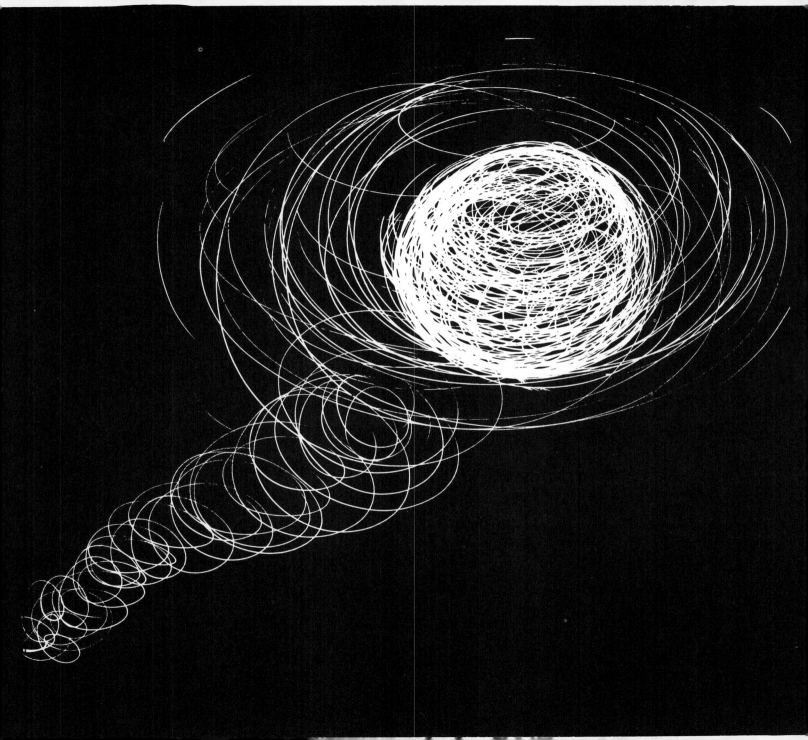

All masses of particles which are free to move and which are not pushed or pulled form into round balls. This is the only shape in which all the pressure at every point on the surface is the same.

The Moon is round. So are the planets. The Sun is round, and so are all the other stars.

None of these objects is exactly round. They would be round if they were not pulled by nearby bodies (the Earth pulls upon the Moon, for example, and flattens it somewhat) and if they were not spinning (the Sun spins and so it is somewhat flattened). Earth spins too, and so our planet is not a perfect sphere. It is a bit fatter around the equator (the middle of the Earth) than it is from pole to pole. If you could slice through the Earth and measure its diameter from North Pole to South Pole, the distance would be 12 714 kilometers (7,899 miles). The diameter at the equator would be 12 757 kilometers (7,926 miles).

It is proper to say that Earth is a round ball, a sphere. But if you wish to be completely accurate, Earth is actually an ''oblate spheroid''—a flattened sphere. And the amount of flattening is one part in about 297.

When artificial satellites first went around the Earth, it was noticed that they did not move evenly. The movement of an earth-circling satellite is affected by the mass of Earth. If the mass were distributed evenly, the satellite would move evenly. But careful measurements indicated that there is more mass south of the equator than north of it. Earth is an oblate spheroid, but it is also somewhat fatter in its southern part. The variation from a smooth oblate spheroid amounts to only a few yards.

When you know the size of something, you can figure out its volume. For example, the volume of the room you are in right now is found by multiplying the length of the room by its width, and then by its height. When the diameter of a sphere is known, you can find its volume. The volume of Earth, the space enclosed by it, is about 1 083 320-000 000 cubic kilometers (259,000,000,000 cubic miles).

VOLUME = LENGTH TIMES WIDTH TIMES HEIGHT

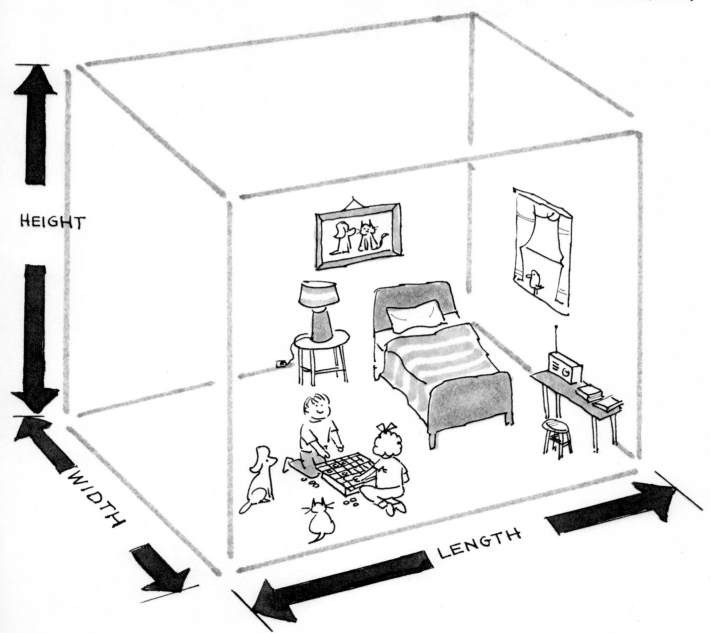

HEIGHT

WIDTH

LENGTH

But Earth is not empty. It contains metals, rocks, soil, water, minerals of all kinds. The material of the Earth appears to be divided into layers. At the center of Earth there is a core of solid nickel and iron that is probably about 2 560 kilometers (1,600 miles) across—800 miles in radius. Around this is a layer of liquid iron that may be 3 200 kilometers (2,000 miles) deep. Around the liquid metal is a layer of solid rock called olivine. This layer may be 2 880 kilometers (1,800 miles) thick. (This adds up to 15 360 kilometers, or 9,600 miles, more than the diameter of the Earth. That's because scientists don't know exactly how thick each layer is.) The surface of the Earth, the part we know, is a crust only 16 to 40 kilometers (10 to 25 miles) thick. If Earth were an apple, the crust would be thinner than the skin of the apple.

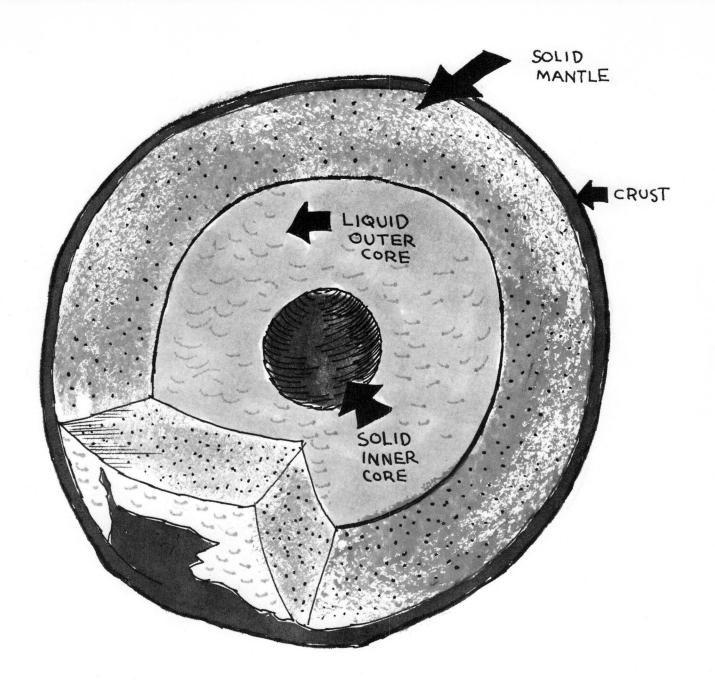

SOLID MANTLE

CRUST

LIQUID OUTER CORE

SOLID INNER CORE

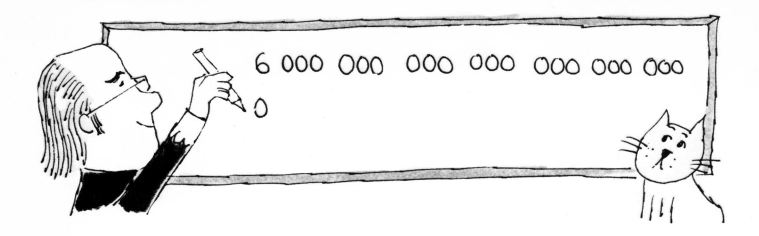

6 000 000 000 000 000 000 000 000 000 0

How much material does Earth contain? What is its mass? Less than two hundred years ago an English scientist, Henry Cavendish, figured it out. He devised a delicate experiment that enabled him to measure the gravitational attraction between two very small metal balls. This gave him a yardstick for figuring out the mass of larger objects, even of the whole Earth. He found it to be 6 000 000 000 000-000 000 000 000 000 grams. It's almost impossible to read such a number, so scientists write it 6×10^{27}. They say, "Six times ten to the twenty-seven." That means 6 followed by 27 zeroes. (The mass of Earth in tons is 6.6×10^{21}.)

Earth is a huge, massive planet—one that moves in many different ways at the same time. One of the first things the Omegan astronomer would notice about our planet is its rotation. This is the motion that we are most aware of, too.

Earth started rotating when it first began. The motion of each separate particle that joined together to make the Earth was transmitted to the new-forming mass. Therefore, the entire mass was spinning. Since there has been no force to stop this spinning, except the slight effect of the tides, Earth has rotated from west to east for billions of years. And it will continue to rotate for billions of years in the future.

Right now the planet is moving some 1 600 kilometers an hour (1,000 m.p.h.) at the equator. A day, reckoned as twenty-four hours long, is the time required for Earth to complete a single rotation. During its history there have probably been times when the Earth rotated faster; and at other times it may have rotated more slowly.

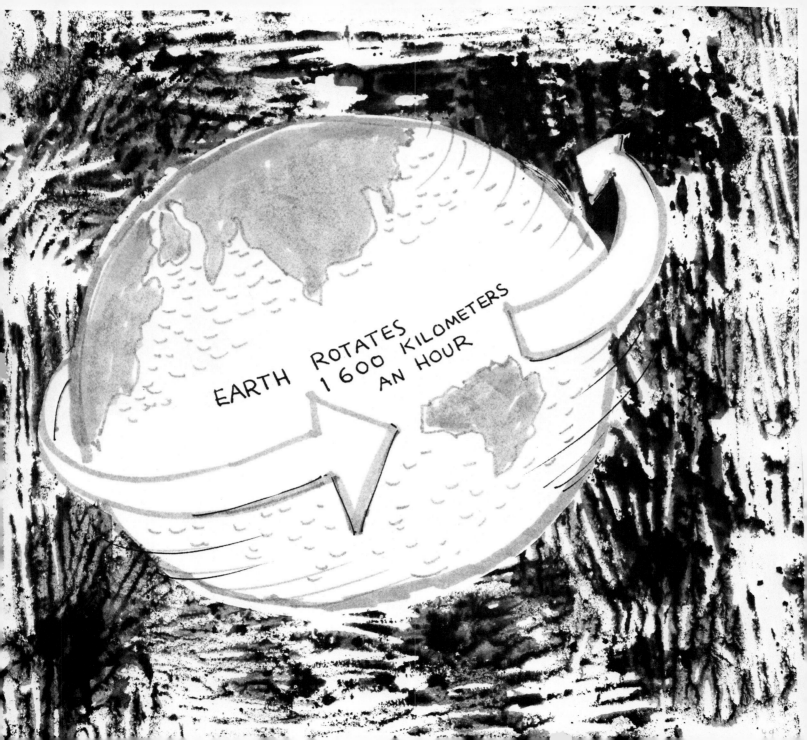

We know Earth rotates because astronauts have watched it from the Moon. They have seen Earth turn, and watched parts of it move into sunlight while other parts moved into shadow.

But even before astronauts went to the Moon and looked back upon the Earth, we knew that our planet was spinning.

Our senses tell us that Earth is standing still, for we have no feeling of the speed of rotation. Instead the stars appear to move from east to west. The Sun seems to move upward in the morning, and downward in the evening. We still talk about sunrise, and sunset. But actually the stars do not move from east to west; the Sun neither rises nor sets. It is the turning of the Earth that makes these things appear to happen. The Sun is always "rising" at some place on the Earth.

In 1851 a Frenchman named Jean Bernard Léon Foucault devised an experiment to prove that Earth rotates, and that sunrise and sunset are due to Earth's turning.

In a building in Paris he hung a weight from a high ceiling. The weight was suspended on a very good bearing, one that had practically no friction. Extending from the weight was a needle. The needle cut a track in a pan of sand as the weight swung back and forth. Hour after hour the path that the needle cut changed. The path turned clockwise. Foucault said that the weight was swinging as though it were fixed in space. If it were lined

up with objects outside the Earth—stars, for example—it would always be lined up with the same stars. Therefore, changes in the path of the needle could be due only to the turning of the Earth. Foucault's experiment proved that Earth was indeed rotating. And it was rotating at such a speed that one turn was completed in twenty-four hours.

The equipment for the experiment was called Foucault's pendulum. You can see pendulums like this at various museums and cultural centers such as the Franklin Institute in Philadelphia, the United Nations building in New York City, and the Museum of Science and Industry in Chicago.

Because Earth rotates we have a succession of day and night. Right now there are twenty-four hours in our days—twenty-four hours from midnight to midnight. If Earth rotated more rapidly, our days would be shorter. The planet Jupiter rotates much faster than Earth does. Days on Jupiter are only ten hours long. If Earth rotated more slowly, our days would be longer. For example, a day on Mercury is fifty-nine Earth-days long. Mercury rotates very slowly.

JUPITER ROTATES
VERY FAST

MERCURY ROTATES
VERY SLOWLY.
A DAY IS VERY
VERY LONG
ON MERCURY

The air that surrounds our planet and the water that covers a large part of it are carried along by the planet. Because they are not attached, the air and water move continually as the Earth turns. Cold air is pulled toward the center of the Earth by gravity. It digs under the warmer air. Cold water sinks to the bottom of the sea. It digs under the warmer water. Movement beneath the warmer air and water causes the cold air and water to move toward the equator. As the cold air becomes heated, it is pushed upward and flows away from the equator in upper-air streams. As the cold water becomes heated, it is pushed upward and flows away from the equator as upper-ocean currents.

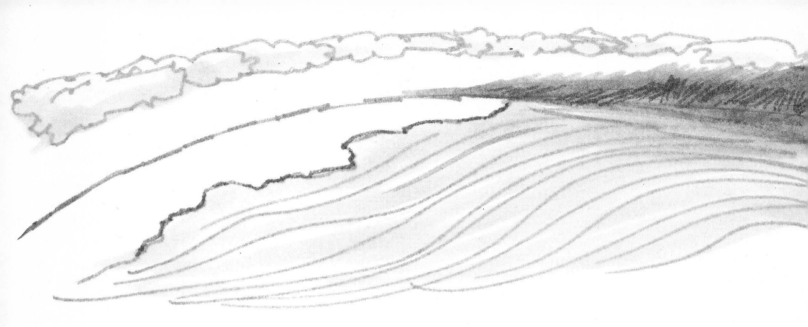

The rotation of the Earth, plus the north and south movements of air and water, cause the air and water to move to the right in the northern half of the Earth and to the left in the southern half. These movements make currents in the seas. One current is the Gulf Stream. It is a "river" of warm water in the Atlantic Ocean that moves from the equator northward along the east coast of North America, across to the west coast of Europe, and southward again to the equator. The Labrador

current moves southward from Labrador and along the northeast coast of North America. Heavy fogs occur where warm air that hangs over the Gulf Stream meets cool air that hangs over the Labrador current.

Our weather is caused largely by the movement of large air masses, and the directions in which the masses move is determined largely by the rotation of the earth. Winds blow northeastward from the equator. They blow southwestward from northern latitudes.

The atmosphere of Earth is in layers. The lower layer, up to five miles or so, is where weather occurs. It is the region that is heated through contact with the warm Earth, and it is the region that loses heat rapidly when Earth is cold.

High above the weather layer—seven to ten miles or more—are the jet streams. These are air masses that move rapidly, generally from west to east. Airplanes going on eastward flights try to fly high enough to get into a jet stream, where they are carried along by it.

Airplanes on westward flights usually fly at lower altitudes so that they will be below a jet stream. The jet streams probably result from Earth's rotation. They are high enough so that the heating of the surface of the Earth does not affect them.

As Earth rotates, its axis points toward Polaris, the North Star. This is true all through the year, no matter what the season may be. Some people wonder how the axis of Earth can always point toward Polaris. After all, they say, if the lines of the axis in summer and winter are continued out into space, they are parallel. And two parallel lines cannot point to the same object. This is true. But Polaris is very far away—almost 700 light years.

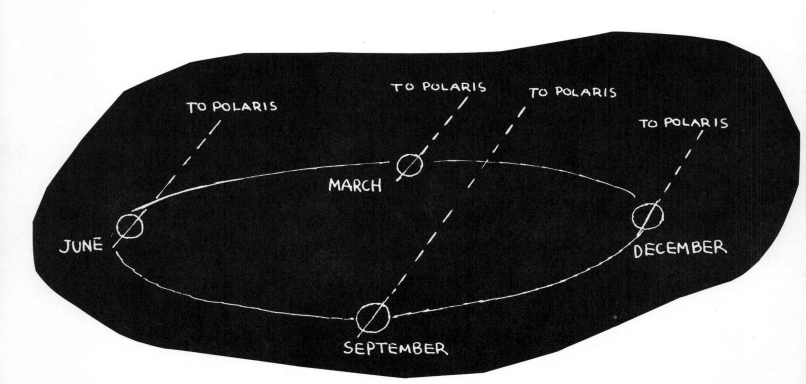

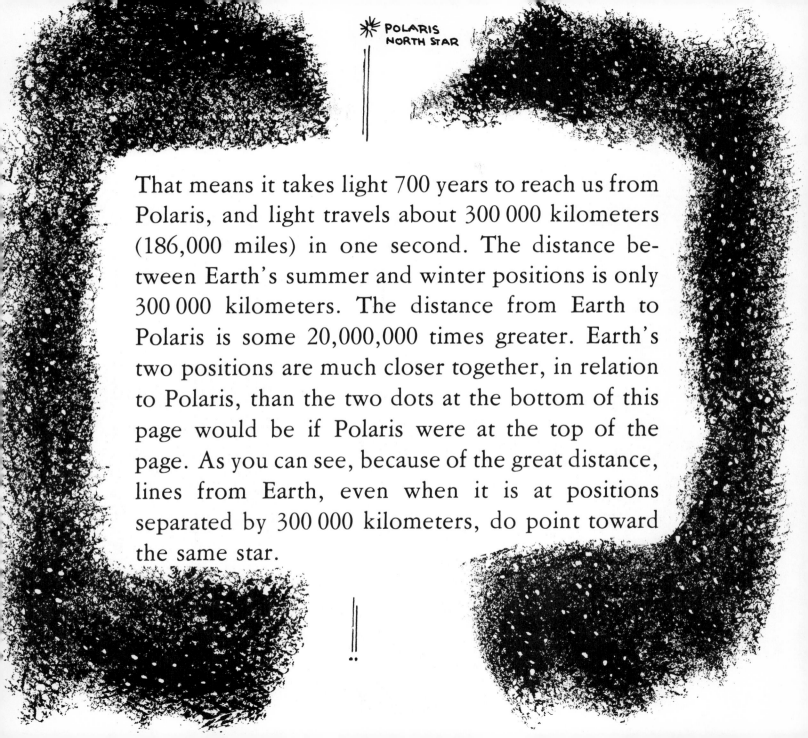

POLARIS
NORTH STAR

That means it takes light 700 years to reach us from Polaris, and light travels about 300 000 kilometers (186,000 miles) in one second. The distance between Earth's summer and winter positions is only 300 000 kilometers. The distance from Earth to Polaris is some 20,000,000 times greater. Earth's two positions are much closer together, in relation to Polaris, than the two dots at the bottom of this page would be if Polaris were at the top of the page. As you can see, because of the great distance, lines from Earth, even when it is at positions separated by 300 000 kilometers, do point toward the same star.

Because Earth's axis is tilted, and because Earth goes around the Sun, the length of daylight and darkness changes at given locations. For example, at the polar regions there are six months of darkness followed by six months of daylight. During most of the six months of darkness the sky is not completely dark. There is some light. But during the entire period the Sun does not come above the horizon. During the six months of daylight the Sun is above the horizon all the time.

Along the equator periods of daylight and darkness are just about the same length all year round. The farther you go from the equator—toward the North Pole or the South Pole—the greater the changes. For example, in most parts of the United States there are fifteen or sixteen hours of daylight in the summer, but only eight or nine hours of daylight in winter.

Because Earth rotates, there is a succession of day and night. Because Earth revolves around the Sun, there are changes in the seasons. The color that Omegan astronomers may observe results from the change of seasons.

Earth revolves around the Sun because it was probably formed out of the same materials that gave birth to the Sun. As the Sun formed from a great mass of dust and gases, so did the Earth. And as the Sun and the Earth formed, they picked up the motion of the gases that made them. The Sun is spinning, the Earth is spinning. The Earth moves around the Sun, so do all the other planets. Very likely they will move around the Sun for billions of years, because there is nothing to stop them from doing so.

PLUTO

Gravitation of the Sun holds the Earth in its orbit. Each second, Earth moves 29.60 kilometers (18.5 miles) along its path, and, at the same time, Earth moves 3 millimeters (¹/₈ inch) toward the Sun. You could say that each second Earth falls 3 millimeters toward the Sun. But since at the same time Earth moves 29.60 kilometers along its path, the two motions result in Earth's moving along a smooth curve, its orbit around the Sun.

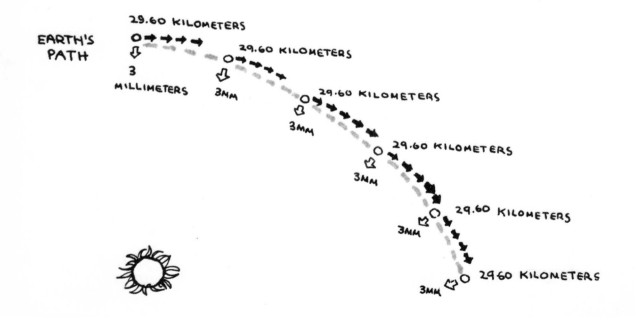

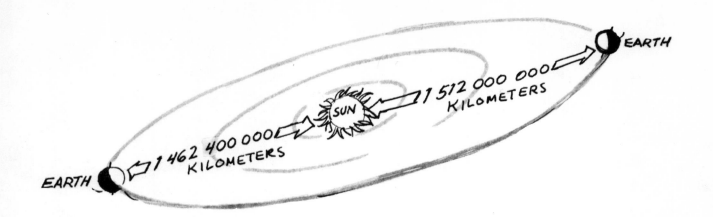

The path is not a circle, however. It is elliptical, a sort of flattened circle. Indeed, the paths of all the planets are elliptical, and so are the paths of the Moon and the other satellites of the Solar System. This means that the distance between the Sun and Earth varies. In July, during summer in the Northern Hemisphere, Earth is farther away from the Sun than it is in January. Around July 4, the distance is 1 512 000 000 kilometers (94,500,000 miles), and around January 5 the distance is 1 462 400 000 kilometers (91,400,000 miles).

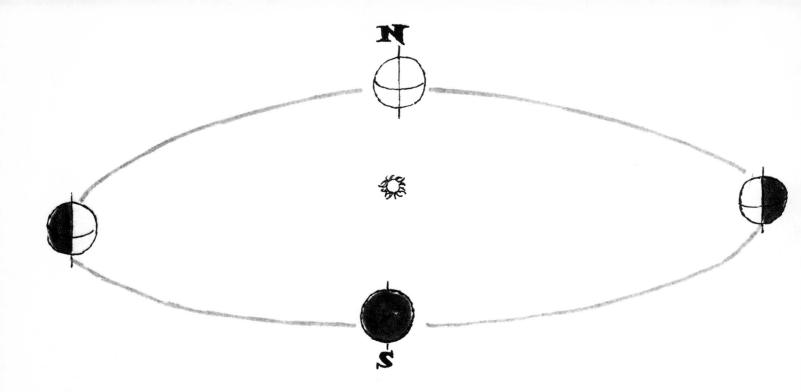

Suppose the axis of Earth were straight up and down in relation to the plane of its orbit. As Earth went around the Sun, the seasons would not change. The weather all through the year would be about as it is during springtime. Suppose the axis were tilted way over. There would be a change of seasons, but the seasons would be quite different from what they are now. In one part of the year the

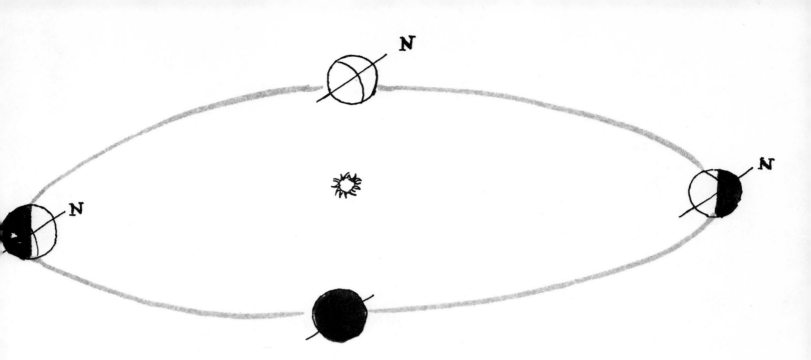

North Pole of the Earth would be pointed almost directly at the Sun. Six months later the same pole would be pointed almost directly away from the Sun. During the year the polar regions would be first very hot and then very cool. The equatorial region of the Earth would receive little sunlight, except during spring and fall, when sunlight would fall directly on the equator.

Because Earth's axis is tilted $23\frac{1}{2}°$, the amount of sunshine that different parts of the Earth receive varies as the year goes by. Sunshine and the tilt of the axis make the seasons.

Have you noticed how the stars and constellations you see seem to change from season to season? In winter in the Northern Hemisphere you see Orion (the Hunter), the Great Dog, and Gemini (the Twins) around nine o'clock in the evening. Six months later you see Cygnus (the Swan), Lyra, and Scorpio about the same time. In any season we see those stars that are in the nighttime sky at that time. Every day of the year all the stars ever seen from your location pass overhead. But you cannot see those that are overhead when the sun is shining. Our sky-view changes with the seasons.

GEMINI

ORION

THE GREAT DOG

WINTER

CYGNUS

LYRA

SCORPIO

SUMMER

As Earth moves around the Sun, it carries the Moon along with it. The Earth pulls on the Moon, and the Moon pulls on the Earth. Earth causes tides on the Moon. There are no ocean tides on the Moon, for there is no water there. But the solid surface of the Moon moves toward the Earth, just as seas on Earth move toward the Moon. The Moon is bulged toward the Earth.

At the same time, the Moon causes tides on the Earth. The seas rise and fall because of the Moon's gravitation. It isn't only the seas that rise and fall; the solid part of Earth does, too. The Moon causes "land tides" that amount to changes of six inches or more. Earth causes "land tides" on the Moon that amount to even greater changes.

IN
26,000
YEARS
EARTH'S AXIS
WILL AGAIN
POINT TO POLARIS

POLARIS
(NORTH STAR)

The pull of the Moon also causes the axis of the Earth to swing about in a large circle. Scientists call this motion "precession." The Moon pulls on the bulge of the earth. This pull would have the effect of straightening Earth's axis if Earth were standing still. But because Earth rotates, the axis resists the force. In so doing, it swings in a wide circle, one that is completed in 26,000 years. Right now the axis points toward Polaris. Ten thousand years from now it will point toward a different part of the sky. But 26,000 years from now the axis will once more point to our present North Star.

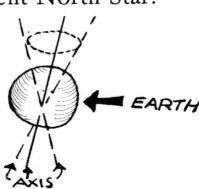

EARTH

AXIS

Earth moves in many ways. It rotates on its axis—some 1 600 kilometers (1,000 miles) per hour. It revolves around the Sun—some 105 600 kilometers (66,000 miles) an hour. It precesses. At the same time Earth moves through space—because it and all the other planets in our Solar System are carried along by the Sun. This is a "motion" that an Omegan astronomer could see quite easily. The Sun is moving toward the constellation Hercules at a speed of 19 kilometers (12 miles) a second, and so are we. Also, the Sun and all its planets share in the motion of the Galaxy of which they are a part. At our location, the Galaxy is rotating at a speed of 24 kilometers a second (150 m.p.s.).

Our Earth moves in many different ways, and at very fast speeds.

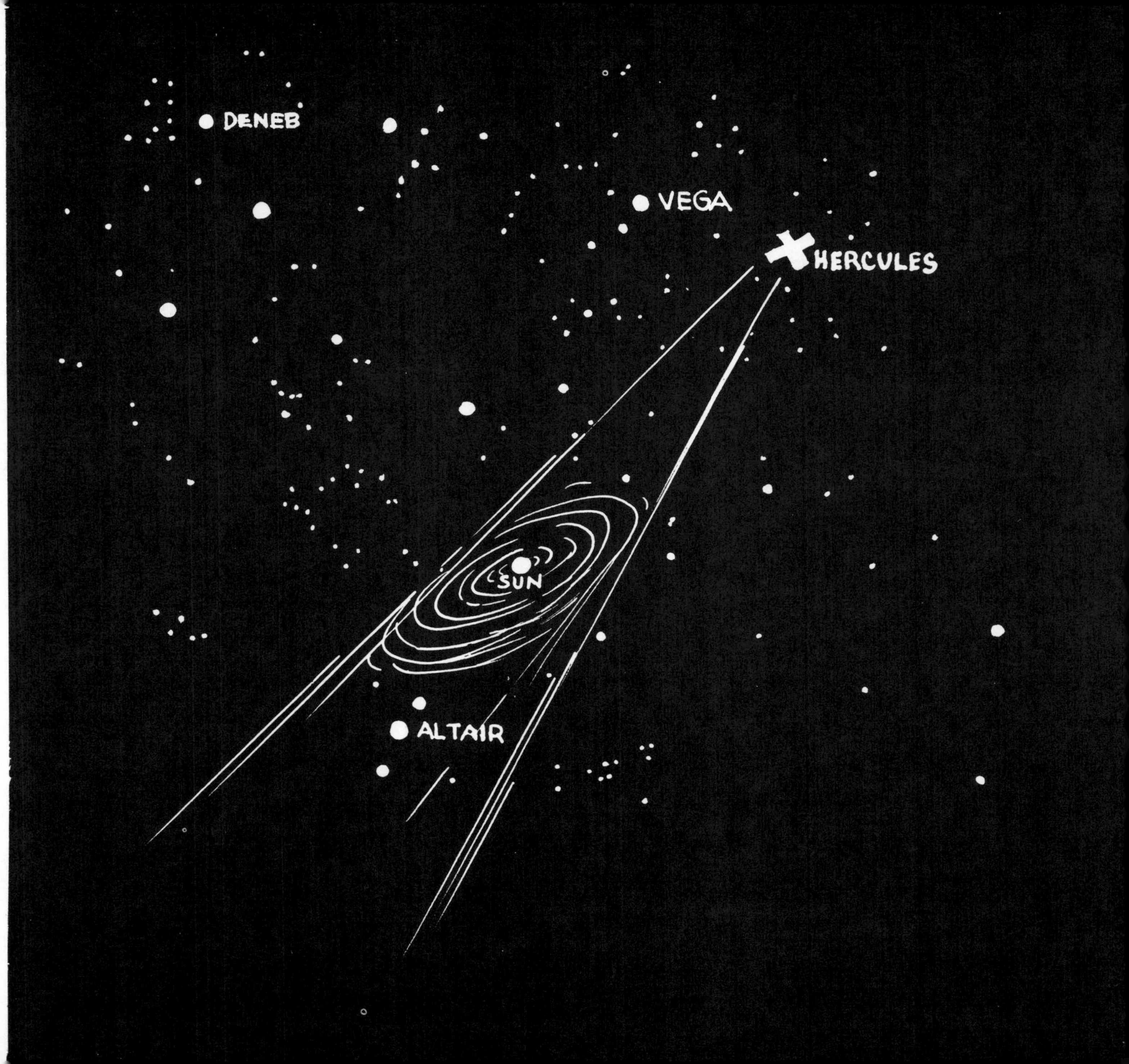
DENEB
VEGA
HERCULES
SUN
ALTAIR

Of all the planets in the Solar System, Earth seems to be the only one that has life upon it. The other planets have not been explored, except by probes that have gone close to Mercury, Venus, Mars, and Jupiter. And instruments have been landed on Venus and Mars. None of these probes has detected any signs of life. But none of them has reached any planet that is beyond our Solar System. So we cannot be sure whether or not there is a planet like Omega somewhere in the universe.

Earth seems to be the only planet that has the water, air, and minerals that life needs in order to appear in the first place, and to continue to grow and flourish. Nearly four billion people live on our planet right now, using the air, water, and minerals. Also, there are untold numbers of plants and animals on the land, in the sea, and in the air.

Earth is surrounded by a layer of gases that make up its atmosphere. The other planets also have atmospheres, but their atmospheres are made of carbon dioxide, or hydrogen, or methane and ammonia, gases that animals cannot use. Our atmosphere, mostly nitrogen and oxygen, extends for a hundred miles or so above us. The atmosphere is an ocean of air, and man is a creature that can survive only at the lower levels of that ocean. Air seems to be very light, so light that we are not aware of it except when the wind blows. But if all the air were put on a scale, it would weigh 4 500-000 000 000 000 metric tons (5×10^{15} short tons).

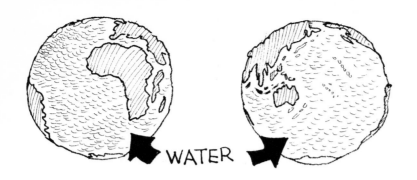

WATER

From outer space, water is the most obvious substance on our planet. What the astronauts' photographs show is the blueness of the water, and the whiteness of the clouds. If there are creatures observing Earth from some other world such as Omega, they might be calling our world the Blue Planet, or perhaps the Water Planet. Three quarters of Earth's surface is covered with water, so continents look like islands floating in the Earth-circling sea. There is so much more water than land that if the surface of Earth were entirely smooth, the water would cover the whole planet.

Biologists tell us that water is the one ingredient that is really necessary for life. Therefore, when explorations for the presence of life are made elsewhere in the universe, water is the substance that scientists look for. It is believed that without water life could not begin anywhere. And we all know that without water life could not go on. Every day we need water. After only three days without water men would perish. And without water other animals, and plants too, could not survive.

Living things also need air, or at least the oxygen in air. In addition, they need minerals from the soil, and the food that grows in the soil. Our planet is about 12 800 kilometers (8,000 miles) across, yet plants and animals can exist on only a tiny fraction of it. There are some creatures on the bottom of the deep seas—say 8 kilometers (5 miles) down. And there are also some at the tops of high mountains—say 7 kilometers (4 to 5 miles) up. So we say that life can survive only in a thin layer of the crust of the Earth—about 15 kilometers (9 to 10 miles). Using an apple to represent the Earth, the area we live in is a layer much thinner than a microscopic layer of the skin of the apple.

Earth is unique in the Solar System. None of the other planets is the same size as ours, none moves as we move, and none has the same seasonal changes that we have. There is no planet that is at the same distance from our Sun, and so there is no planet that has the same temperature that Earth has. Also, there is no planet that has an ocean of oxygen and nitrogen surrounding it, oceans of water upon it, and a thin layer of soil in which plants may grow.

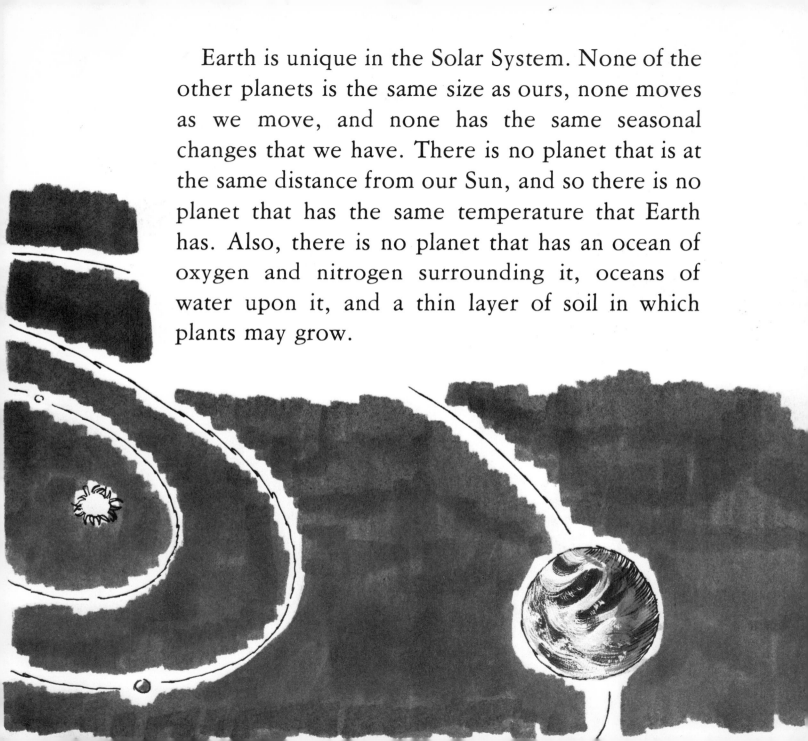

Earth is the only one of the nine planets that is teeming with life, the only planet where man or intelligent creatures of any kind exist.

But there may be other planets going around distant stars of our Galaxy—or of galaxies beyond our own. Perhaps Omega does exist somewhere, and perhaps Omegan astronomers, who breathe air just as we do, are looking at us right now, trying to learn more about the strange blue-white world that they see dimly in their super telescopes.

ABOUT THE AUTHOR

Franklyn M. Branley, Astronomer Emeritus and former Chairman of The American Museum—Hayden Planetarium, is well known as the author of many books about astronomy and other sciences for young people of all ages. He is also the coeditor of the Let's-Read-and-Find-Out Science books.

Dr. Branley holds degrees from New York University, Columbia University, and the State University of New York College at New Paltz. He and his wife live in Woodcliff Lake, New Jersey, and spend their summers in Sag Harbor, New York.

ABOUT THE ILLUSTRATOR

Leonard Kessler is a writer and illustrator of children's books as well as a designer and painter. He became interested in children's books as a result of teaching art to young people.

Mr. Kessler was born in Akron, Ohio, but he moved east to Pittsburgh at an early age. He was graduated from Carnegie-Mellon University with a degree in fine arts, painting, and design. He lives in New City, New York, in Rockland County.

ABOUT THE CONSULTANT

Professor X2L754(YY) is Chairperson of the Extra-Omegan Studies Group, and developer of the remarkable macrotelescope which has made it possible for Omegan scientists to observe distant solar systems. Holder of the highest degree from Alphaville University, in Omega's capital city, and well known for his research in hyperdensity, Professor (YY) has been a member of the Grearlidge Commune for the past ninety-six years.